THE GIRL WHO WAS HER BROTHER'S KEEPER

THE LOVE BEYOND LIFE

BROTHER PRATER

authorHOUSE®

AuthorHouse™
1663 Liberty Drive
Bloomington, IN 47403
www.authorhouse.com
Phone: 833-262-8899

Published by AuthorHouse 07/27/2020

ISBN: 978-1-7283-6770-5 (sc)
ISBN: 978-1-7283-6778-1 (e)

Library of Congress Control Number: 2020913323

Print information available on the last page.

Any people depicted in stock imagery provided by Getty Images are models, and such images are being used for illustrative purposes only. Certain stock imagery © Getty Images.

This book is printed on acid-free paper.

CONTENTS

Forwarded by vii

Introduction ix

Disclaimer xi

Chapter 1   Boy Meets Girl 1

Chapter 2   Time for School 6

Chapter 3   2 Curious Kids 9

Chapter 4   There's a New Sheriff in Town 10

Chapter 5   Hanging with My Hero! 14

Chapter 6   We Got Each Other's Back 17

Chapter 7   Enough is Enough 18

Chapter 8   Beauty, Brains, & a Big Mouth 19

Chapter 9   June & Sheila Plus One 25

Chapter 10   Same Song but Different Verse 28

Chapter 11   Searching for Love 30

Chapter 12   The Break-Up 32

Chapter 13   The Make- Up 33

Chapter 14   Speaking it to Existence 34

Chapter 15   The Big Day is Here 36

Chapter 16   Sheila's True Love 38

Chapter 17   Sheila & Her Savior 39

Chapter 18   Just Being Big Kids 42

Chapter 19   Our Last Dance 45

Chapter 20   The Day I Lost A Part of Me! 48

Chapter 21   Facing the World, ALONE! 50

Chapter 22   Just Shut Up! 52

Chapter 23   The Day I Say Goodbye 53

Since You've Been Gone 57

FORWARDED BY:

DERRICK RICHARDSON

It moves me greatly to once again be accounted part of the anointed writings of Brother Prater. He not only has a passion for the church and people of God, but also people of every ethnic group and background. I have witnessed his ministry fruitfully grow and spread rapidly throughout the years, as his integrity as a man and minister has impeccably stood the process. I have known him for over thirty years, and twenty of those as a born-again believer. I have witnessed his ups and his downs. I have witnessed his character in times of victory, and I have witnessed his character in his times of despair.

Brother Prater has always stood the test and prevailed. His character through it all has never wavered, has stood firm, never changing, stays constant and steady while gracefully enduring it all. His church ministry has blessed many, as he has sacrificially shown that faithfulness to leaders and flocks is still very much acceptable in God's eyes. His social media ministry reaches masses across the globe, as souls from far and near have connected with his ministry to experience God's best for them. His gifts are sharp and on point. His speech is graceful and seasoned. His calling is evident.

His current writing of this book is an overwhelmingly heart felt endearment. At the same time, it reaches down into our spiritual bowels. It will uplift the inner man that is sometimes captive to this world, and it's inevitable seasons of sorrow, mourning, and grief.

To whom Brother Prater dedicates this book, I knew her as well. I could only imagine what my dear brother's journey was like at the discovery of Sheila Prater's passing. Sheila herself was a very strong and solid African American Queen. Sheila has always stood her ground to the absolute fullest, and man o man would she stand in strength to protect and cover her brother. Their bond was beyond the norm, as they shared a friendship as strong as covenant partnership. That brotherly and sisterly union and bond can never physically be relived. My catalog of fond memories of their bond will always live.

Brother Prater has chosen to totally reveal his transparency as well as vulnerabilities in this current writing. Thus, God has once again given Brother Prater the platform to reach the masses through his personal experience. Any man who titles his book "The Girl Who was Her Brother's Keeper", exemplifies the character of a humble and great man. This further expresses to Brother Prater's submission to God's plans for every endeavor of God's purpose in his life.

INTRODUCTION

Some people said that they had a guardian angel looking down from heaven upon them, but my guardian angel was different. She grew up with me, went to school with me & stood up to bullies for me. That guardian angel was my sister, Sheila Prater.

Sheila always made it a point to come to my rescue, even if I didn't need her to. Even though I was older than her (by 362 days), we considered ourselves twins. Our close bond & crazy conversations were always enjoyed by others, especially on social media. Regardless of how things were, she always had my back. She was a great support to me as a minister & as a brother. I could always count on her. Sadly, March 3, 2019, Sheila was killed by homicide.

That day, my whole life changed. I didn't know how I was going to live my life without her, but God led me to write this book about my life with her.

Me & Sheila

DISCLAIMER

As I share the life journey of Sheila & I, I pray that this book will minister to people everywhere & encourage them to develop a close relationship with their sibling(s). So often, we take our siblings for granted thinking that their feelings aren't important, their opinions don't matter or hold on to grudges over matters that means absolutely NOTHING! We plan for our siblings to be with us forever, but death can come at any time to snatch them away from you. This may lead to a life full of regrets, guilt or you may have missed an opportunity of having a great friend within them.

Just know that the things that are of great value take prayers & hard work to achieve, & relationships (especially within the family) are very valuable! It may need someone such as you to be THE ONE who God uses to bring changes within your family. But even if you do everything possible & it still doesn't work out, God will bless you & give you peace for doing what He told you to do. You just have to continue to pray for them & be obedient to God about that matter. Remember, your obedience will give God ACCESS to that situation as He encourages you. Who knows? Your prayers may be the difference maker that reaches them, so please.... DON'T STOP PRAYING!

CHAPTER 1

BOY MEETS GIRL

The most important celebration for a business is that 1ˢᵗ year anniversary because it sets the tone for the rest of the years that follow it. Well, 3 days before the 1ˢᵗ year anniversary of my birth, my sister Sheila Prater was born & came home 3 days later.... ON MY 1ˢᵗ BIRTHDAY. Think about it, I got my sister Sheila for my 1ˢᵗ birthday gift. WOW! God must have known that I was going to need her in my life.

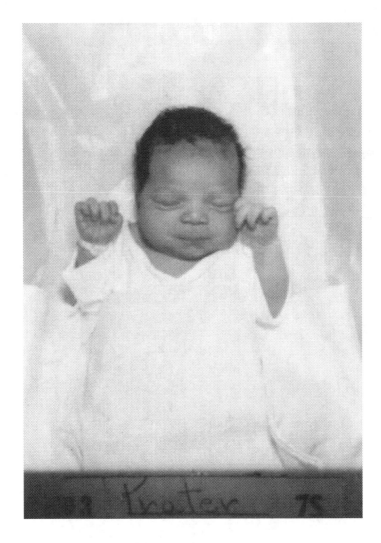

Sheila Prater (1973)

Me & Sheila (1974)

I was told that when we were babies, when one of us cried, the other one cried too. From my earliest memory as a child, it was always about Sheila & I. You wouldn't see one without the other. We were never lonely or bored because we would always entertain each other. We watched the same shows, slept in the same bed, & did everything the other would do. I quickly learned that she was the smarter one.

And if you didn't believe it, she would have told you herself. Sheila was the 1st one to learn how to blow a bubblegum & tie her own shoes! When she found out that I didn't know how to tie my shoes, she took me to our brothers' room, sat on our oldest brother's (Jerry) bed & showed me how to do it. It seemed like an eternity, but eventually, I did it.

Since we were on Jerry's bed, we decided to celebrate by jumping on it! We thought that jumping on Jerry's bed was the best that we could get revenge on him since he used to make us take early naps & whoop us. If we couldn't get to him, at least we got to his bed.

We were the kids' version of Donny & Marie Osmond. People used to ask us if we were twins. One of us would say, "No! We're 362 days apart." People called us Mutt & Jeff, because we were stuck together like glue.

Sheila & I (1977)

CHAPTER 2

TIME FOR SCHOOL

One day, my mom took Sheila & I to the elementary school across the street from our house. When we got there, I noticed that mama was just filling out paperwork with my information & not Sheila's. When I asked mama why, she told me that I was qualified to start school because of my age, but Sheila wasn't. I was heartbroken! Even though my 2nd older brother Ronnie was going to the same school as a 6th grader, it was not the same as having my sidekick, Sheila, with me.

When the 1st day of school came, I was a nervous wreck. For the 1st time, Sheila & I were going to be apart. I was NOT looking forward to it. Mama got us dressed so I could be dropped off. When we finished getting dressed, mama drove us to the school. We made it to the school & arrived at Mrs. Smallwood's kindergarten class. As I'm walking into the classroom, I turned around & saw Sheila's face at the door. She had a grin hiding a sad face. I wish I knew what to say to have to make her feel better, but I felt just as bad as her. As the bell rang for class to start, mama & Sheila began to walk away. Sheila walked a few steps & turned around to look at me. I kept staring at her until she eventually waved & walked away.

During class, I thought that all the other kids were going to be nice like Sheila. Boy, was I wrong! There was a boy named Chris who untied my shoes & would not tie them back. He made me so mad that I wanted to punch him. That one bad act that Chris did ruined my day. When I got picked up from school, I couldn't wait until I told Sheila. I told her everything & was just glad to be home.

The next morning, mama woke me up to get ready for school. "School?" I thought school was just for 1 day. I told my family, "I'm NOT going back to school! I'm staying home to be with Sheila!" My parents thought I was kidding until I started taking off my clothes & I messed up my hair. This went on for a few minutes until I got a whooping. Afterwards, my mama fixed my clothes, my daddy combed my hair & put me into the car. While my mama was driving, I jumped out the car & ran back home. When I made it back home, my parents **STRONGLY** convinced me (with a belt named Black Beauty) to **NEVER** do that mess again. I got sent back to school & thought about that whooping all school year long!

The next school year came. This time, I'm in the 1st grade & Sheila arrives at the kindergarten. Yes! We were finally in school together. She was also enrolled in Mrs. Smallwood's class, just like me. After suffering last school year without her, I have her with me now.

Even though we wouldn't be in the same class, at least she was up there. I could handle that! After a few weeks of school, some of the school's staff wanted to have a meeting with our parents about Sheila. She was so smart that they asked our parents if they would like for her to be advanced to the 1st grade. As our mom & daddy were discussing it, Sheila said that she wanted to be in the 1st grade, so her & I could be in the same grade. Our parents approved it. So, now it's official... Sheila's in the 1st grade with me!

Sheila (1980)

CHAPTER 3

2 CURIOUS KIDS

Sheila & I were typical kids. We played with bugs, dug up dirt & played hopscotch. Whatever we did, we did together. I was always curious about things. I had a children's Picture Bible that Jerry got for me. I was blown away by the story of Jesus' crucifixion & being raised from the dead. I told Sheila that I had an idea & if God was really real, He's going to prove it.

My idea was to get my G. I. Joe action figure, make him go through the crucifixion, bury him & God was going to raise it up. Sheila thought that it was crazy, but she was willing to help anyway. I got my G.I. Joe, beat it, took all its clothes, wrapped it in a white handkerchief, nailed it to a cross made of sticks, & put red jelly on its eyes. I went to the backyard & placed the cross to the ground for a couple hours.

After a few hours, I went outside to bury the G.I. Joe. I buried it in a specific spot of the backyard. As soon as I finished, I walked into the house & immediately... it started thundering & raining.

After the 3rd day, I told Sheila to follow me to the backyard. I grabbed a shovel & went where I buried the G. I. Joe. I shoveled at the spot, around the spot & away from the spot where G.I. Joe was, & G.I. JOE WAS GONE! Sheila saw it for herself, she screamed out, "GOD IS REAL!" That moment became a moment we would never forget... God revealed His Power for 2 little curious kids.

CHAPTER 4

THERE'S A NEW
SHERIFF IN TOWN

It was really great for Sheila & I to be in school together. We had the same grade, lunch period & got out of school at the same time. That's awesome! The time we lost last year because she wasn't in school yet, was being made up this year by us hanging out at school & home. But as our lives were back to the way it used to be, our parents gave us the news that would change our lives forever… OUR MAMA WAS PREGNANT! WHAT???!!? PREGNANT!?! And she's having a boy. This was something that Sheila & I did not plan for! Now we're trying to put our heads together to figure out what we're going to do with having a baby in the house. We came up with the idea of giving our soon-to-be little brother a trial period. If he behaves, then he'll be included into the family. But if all he's going to do is cry, then we're going to take him to mama & make her send him back to where he came from.

As the months went by, Sheila & I were making the most of the time we had as the youngest of the family. We would be in our bedroom taking turns driving our imaginary cars, playing grocery store or just talking. When we were done, we would be glued to the tv to watch some of our favorite shows like Sesame Street, the Electric Company, or What's Happening. Even at our young age, we had some deep questions in our little minds. We would watch shows or look up stuff, so we could help to raise our little brother, so he wouldn't be bad.

One Thursday afternoon, while we were in school, I was called to the principal's office. I was scared. I thought I was in trouble. When I made it to the office, Sheila was there. The office staff told us that our daddy was picking us up because our mama was in the hospital with the baby. It's official, we are no longer the babies of the family.

Saturday afternoon, daddy, Sheila & I went to the hospital to pick up mama & our little brother. When we 1st saw him, we thought the hospital switched the baby. He was very white. But I told Sheila that maybe they gave us the baby that wouldn't cry, so we won't say nothing & keep the white baby we have. She thought that made sense. So, we kept that to ourselves!

Prater Family (1983)

Prater Kids (1983)

CHAPTER 5

HANGING WITH MY HERO!

Since our family had gotten bigger, it gave Sheila & I more responsibilities. It grew us up fast. We were tackling adult problems in a kids' body. But no matter what the tasks were, we did them together.

By having more responsibilities, I saw Sheila's strengths & skills. She was the more social one & the better communicator, while I was the quiet sidekick & worker. I saw her leadership skills take center stage. And if we were deciding between her idea or mine, most of the time, I would go along with hers.

I knew that I had to make her the leader of the June & Sheila's Club. If we were a famous duo, Sheila was Batman & I was Robin; She was Bert & I was Ernie; She was Albert, I was Costello; she was Ethal & I was Lucy or She was Morris Day & I was Jerome. I had no problem taking the backseat, so Sheila could drive into the spotlight. She was the perfect fit for the job.

People used to tell us that we looked alike & that made us want to look like each other even more. We would go into the bathroom to get on the scale to see each other's weight. We used to sing together. Because my voice was a high pitch, Sheila & I used to sing together in unison. One day, we came with the idea of how to keep our looks the same forever. We didn't want our noses to get big, so we would keep a clothes pin on our noses as we were around the house & pinch our noses when we had to yawn or sneeze. Also, if we had to clean our noses, we always use tissue & only use the tip of our pinky fingernail (just the tip) to clean it out. The rule was... *NEVER* use your index finger because it will make your nose hole bigger & it will continue to grow forever.

I figured that since Sheila was the better looking of the 2, I wanted to have my eyes, teeth, & complexion like her. I used to get a fingernail file to file my teeth for them to look like hers. We both started using skin whitening to match our complexion even more, & wash my mouths with jewelry cleaner to have whiter teeth. But the most painful experience was when I wanted to have the same color eyes as Sheila's. I figured that if a person would stay in the sun to tan their skin, all I needed to do was to go outside (when it was extremely hot) & stare at the sun as long as I could, so it could tan my eyes. Geesh! That was a ***HUGE*** mistake.

As close as her & I were, the main pet peeve we had was never eating or drinking from someone else. That was a major no, no! We didn't do it from each other & we definitely wouldn't do it from somebody else. Even at home, if one of us walked away from their drink & a sibling drank some of it, the other person would throw it away. It was considered contaminated.

CHAPTER 6

WE GOT EACH OTHER'S BACK

Inside the June & Sheila's Club, we knew that we had each other's back. Whenever somebody tried to bully me at school, Sheila would always appear from out of nowhere to stick up for me. If a boy was trying to pick on her, before I could get in the action to save the day, Sheila would already have the boy on the ground bleeding. That girl was tougher than Superman's kneecaps.

Sheila & I would always make sure that before we would go out in public, that we would inspect each other's appearance. Besides checking each other's clothes & hair to make sure everything was in place, we would check each other's noses to make sure that it was clean. So, we would embarrass each other in public, I made up a code. We would say, "Your "N" not "C". That means "Your Nose Not Clean". To make sure that nobody knew what we were talking about, we would make sure that we said it very fast. When you say it really fast, it sounds like you're saying, "You're Nancy!"

Sheila & I made a covenant (or oath) to be together & to take care of each other. Now, it was not uncommon for people to have a covenant with each other. In 1Samuel 18:3, Jonathan made a covenant with his friend & future king David. Also, in Ruth 1:16-18, we see Ruth vowed to Naomi. We wanted our bond to be unbreakable. That's why we created a policy: We were NOT accepting any applications to join our club. No one could apply for a membership. We have reached our limit! Just June & Sheila!

CHAPTER 7

ENOUGH IS ENOUGH

There were times that the pressures of home & school were weighing on Sheila & I. One day, we went to our bedroom to talk. We decided that we were going to run away together. We didn't have a clue about anything outside of the house or school. We figured that since we were going to be together, everything else would work itself out. I remember watching tv seeing kids get a pole, pack their stuff, put it in a bandana, & leave. I figured, that was the rule to run away. I went to the backyard. I didn't see any poles, so I grabbed 2 big sticks. We didn't have any bandanas, so I went into the bathroom & got 2 of our mama's big towels. Sheila had already grabbed some clothes, so we put them in the towel. We figured that we would get hungry along the way, so I made a couple of bologna sandwiches & put them with our stuff.

After we got all of our stuff together, we wrapped it up, put it under the bed. We headed to our daddy so we could tell him that we were running away. Sheila & I stopped daddy in the hallway & told him that we needed to talk. We told him that we thanked him for raising us but now we're grown (I was about 9, Sheila was about 8) & we were going to run away. He asked us where we were going. We told him that we didn't know yet. Daddy (in his patient & calm voice) told us not to go. After he spoke to us for some minutes, he convinced us to stay home. We went back to our room, unpacked everything & ate those bologna sandwiches.

CHAPTER 8

BEAUTY, BRAINS, &
A BIG MOUTH

Sheila's Beauty

During our time in school, Sheila was considered one of the good-looking girls at the school. She was just a natural pretty girl. Everybody always complimented her on her smile. Although she was not allowed to wear make-up early, she was always told that she didn't need it. She was a sharp dresser too. I would be with her as she was matching up clothes to put together. She knew how to make clothes match together.

Sheila always had her hair on point. Our mom would do both of our hairs. Sheila & I used to look forward to Saturday nights. That was when our mama would part & grease our hair, then part the stocking over our heads to moisturize our hair (Today's time, people use a wave cap). Our favorite part of the stocking was the leg part, where you tie a knot on one side of it. I didn't like the toe part of it, but Sheila would take turns with me, so I could have the knot end sometimes. After we would get up & dressed for church, mama would always hot comb our hair. Sheila's hair would always stay neat, but my hair would shrink the second I started sweating.

Sheila's Brain

Sheila could figure out problems without writing them down. She was very good with numbers, even at an early age. When we used to play with toy cash registers or toy phones, it was helping her to learn the 10- keys by touch, so she could eventually become the secretary. If she answered the phone & was taking a message, she would remember the person's name, number & message. That girl's memory was so good, if you promised her something, she wouldn't forget.

Guys would always try to get to her by trying to become friends with me. Even though I had no clue, Sheila could see right through their con games. She was very smart beyond her years. Sheila was very observant & could grasp things fast. She could multitask too. She could do her homework, listen to the radio, talk on the phone, watch tv & pass her homework with an A+. But me? Shoots! I could study, have the radio off, t.v. off, drink Holy Water, have a prayer vigil & still only get a C-. Even in Sheila's busy time with school, piano lessons or cheerleading, she would always have time to help me with my homework.

One year, Sheila & I were in the same English class. She sat right behind me. She looked out for me with my classwork, so I could raise my grades up. I trusted Sheila & my grades moved from C's to A-'s. One particular time, we were going to do a test in class. I figured I'd try the classmate who "looked" smart. Sheila told me that she knew all the answers, but I told her, "That's ok! I'm getting it from her!" Well, when we got our grades, Sheila made a 100% & me & that classmate who "looked" smart made a 50%. That taught me to never doubt Sheila's brain again!

Sheila's Mouth

Some guys would look at Sheila & think that they could talk to her in a disrespectful way? ***NOOOO WAY!*** She knew what to say to get her point across & to end any foolishness. Sheila had a powerful way of using her "verbal judo" skills She knew how to put the fear of God in people. Word got out fast that she knew how to hold her own. Even when somebody wanted to bully me, before I could defend myself, ***HERE COMES SHEILA PRATER!*** She would jump in front of me & dare them to do something. They would immediately leave. From that point on, when people saw me, they didn't call me by my name, they would say, "Man! That's Sheila Prater's Brother!"

CHAPTER 9

JUNE & SHEILA PLUS ONE

Sheila hadn't been feeling well for a few days. At the time, her & I were working together at a store. People knew that we were brother & sister. When she started missing work because she was sick, people would ask how she was doing. One night before bedtime, she came to my room to talk. She told me that mama was going to drop me off at school & take her to the doctor. She was telling me her all her symptoms & we were trying to figure out what was wrong. She named several viruses, diseases & other illnesses that I never heard of, but one thing that she made loud & clear was.... **"I KNOW I AIN'T PREGNANT!"** I blew a sigh of relief. Because Sheila said she wasn't, a 2nd thought **NEVER** crossed my mind. If Sheila saying it, **I BELIEVED IT!**

The next morning, I was dropped off to school. A few hours later, I was sitting in my classroom, the door opened & it was Sheila. She asked the teacher for permission to talk to me in the hallway. I walked to the hallway & closed the classroom door. Sheila said (in a quiet voice), "I just wanted to just wanted to tell you... (screaming & crying) *I'M PREGNANT!!!*" I said, "WHAT???" Immediately, every teacher ran out of their classes to see what happened. Sheila repeated again (in a scared voice), "I'm pregnant!" My teacher asked if everything was alright & I told him the news. I was shocked & scared! I asked Sheila, "What we gonna do?" It seemed like I was becoming a father more than an uncle. Although this news came as a surprise, she knew that I would travel this journey with her.

During her pregnancy, I felt every pain that Sheila had. I didn't know if that was because we were so close or if I was being punished. This went on throughout her entire pregnancy. She got bigger & bigger right before my eyes. Even though she was big, she still went to work with me. One September afternoon, Sheila & I were home alone. As I was dressing in my bedroom, Sheila yelled out from her bedroom, "I'm going to have a baby." I said, "Yes! I know you're gonna have a baby." Then Sheila said, "NO! I'm going to have a baby NOW!" "WHAT?!?" I got so nervous that I lost all train of thought. I took my car keys from my pocket, threw it on the table & yelled, "I'm going to work!" I walked right out the house & started walking. So happened that my mom was down the street. She called Sheila & came home to take Sheila to the hospital. She later had a bounding baby boy!

I felt horrible for leaving Sheila & she reminded me of it as soon as I saw her at the hospital. I repeatedly apologized for it & she accepted it. Now, it's time to celebrate her being a new mom & me, a new uncle.

When I returned back to work, there were several people asking if Sheila had her baby yet. I told them, "Yes! It's a boy." This went on all day. To let people know that Sheila had a baby boy without folks asking me, I decided to write on the back of my car window, IT'S A BOY! I went to work with the sign on my car. I still had people asking me. The shocking statement a few people came to me with was, "Did you have a baby boy?" I said, "No ma'am! My sister did!" They said, "Oh! We knew you couldn't have no baby!" What in the heck do you mean by that? Forget it! Have a nice day!

(Photo of Sheila and Baby Trey)

CHAPTER 10

SAME SONG BUT DIFFERENT VERSE

Having this baby home was a totally different experience than when my little brother came home. This one was like having my own son. Sheila was very guarded with him & I was guarded with him & her. Although this was her 1st child, Sheila was handling motherhood like a pro. Maybe the years of baby-sitting as a teen prepared her for this.

As the years passed, Sheila came into my bedroom & told me that she wanted to talk to me. After she came in & sat on the bed, she told me that she was pregnant. I remembered that I fell to my bed. After I sat up, I said, "Well Sheila, we gonna take care of this baby too. And THIS time, I WON'T RUN OUT ON YOU! I PROMISE!"

She had crazy cravings. She would have me go to the store to get some crazy combinations of food. Things that she normally wouldn't eat, were now the regular menu items she wanted.

Just like the 1st pregnancy, I felt the pains that Sheila had. Even though I was feeling them, I wanted to watch what I ate, so I wouldn't grow like her. We would walk around the park in front of the house to help with her pregnancy. We did this for many months. Even in her discomfort, Sheila still knew how to be entertaining.

One January Sunday, we came home from church. Sheila said that she was having labor pains. OHHHHH BOY! The last time, I acted like the cowardly lion, but this time.... I'm drinking courage juice! I helped Sheila sit down on the living room couch. While our mom was getting Sheila's clothes, I stayed with Sheila until it was time for her & mom to go. My nephew stayed home with me while his mom was about to make him a brother.

A few hours later, my mom called & said that Sheila gave birth to a girl. OH WOW! Sheila has given birth to a clone of her & I!

Sheila & Tiara

CHAPTER 11

SEARCHING FOR LOVE

Sheila & I always wanted the best for each other in the relationship department. She would screen a potential mate I had my eyes on. She would give me her advice but ultimately tell me that it was my decision. I always felt like meeting ladies was very hard for me. I wasn't a clubby type person. I didn't know where to meet anyone plus, I was too shy to go up to a lady & strike up a conversation.

One night, my friend Paul & I were talking on the phone about finding Ms. Right. I came up with the idea of us calling a phone dating service. This particular free dating service would allow us to listen to the women's profile & if we like them, we would have the option to connect with them live. Paul loved the idea & wanted us to do it.

I made a 3-way call, so Paul could hear & would let me know if he wanted me to connect or dismiss them from our phone line. As times rolled by, I listened to this one particular profile. She caught my attention. It sounded like we had similar interests (Even Paul said that). The more I'd listen to her, the more I wanted to meet her. We had so much in common. I told Paul, "I think I found the perfect girl!" I pressed the button on my phone to connect with her live. We introduced ourselves. Although I was taken aback by her soft sultry voice, she had a recognizable voice that I couldn't put my finger on.

As I continued to ask her question, it hit me where I heard her voice from. I said, "Is this Sheila?" She said, "June? Why you on here" I said, "Why are you on here Sheila? Gurl, get off this dang phone!" Paul asked me if I knew her. I said, "Yes! That's my sister, Sheila!"

Sheila Relaxing

CHAPTER 12

THE BREAK-UP

Although Sheila & I were close, sometimes disagreements happened. One day she got so upset with me, that she didn't want to speak. I didn't know exactly why she was so upset, so I figured I'd call her. She wouldn't answer her phone. Days later, she would eventually call me, only to tell me that she didn't want to talk to me, then she would hang up. I began to pray about it. God told me to write her name down on a piece of paper (SHEILA), then switch the letters E & I (SHIELA). I then noticed that the letters E & L were together. See, EL in Hebrew means God. Then God told me, "Now that I put God in her name, put God in that situation!" Wow! That blew my mind!

Now as I prayed, there was no immediate change. In fact, it looked like things had gotten worse. She would still call me, only to hear me answer, then hang up the phone. I told God about that & He was like, "That's a good thing!" Huh? "Her calling & hanging up in my face is a good thing?" He said, "Yes! It's **HURT** that's making her hang up, but it's **LOVE** that's making her call! So, **Accept** her **LOVE**, but **PRAY** for her **HURT!**" I prayed & prayed until one Sunday afternoon, my phone rung. When I looked at my caller I.D., it was Sheila. I answered the phone as if nothing happened. I said, "Hellllloooo!" She said, "Hi!" I said, "Hey Sheila Prater!" She said, "Hi Junebug!" We had a brief conversation, but I was able to ask her if we could have lunch. I wanted to talk to her. She said YES! When we got off the phone, I thanked God for doing what He could only do.

CHAPTER 13

THE MAKE- UP

The time came for us to meet up. Although plans failed for us to meet in person, Sheila & I talked over the phone for 3 ½ hours! I told her that being away from her or not talking to her was like a bad break-up that you couldn't get over. She shared those same feelings. In the midst of our conversation, God revealed the source of the problem.... a miscommunication. When she understood what happened, she felt bad. She apologized for the miscommunicated & the way she acted. I told her that I forgave her & I love her. I also apologized for my part in the miscommunication & would work on being clearer in my conversations. I was just happy to have my Sheila back into my life. She also promised to never hang up in my face again. Lol!

CHAPTER 14

SPEAKING IT TO EXISTENCE

One night, I was in my bedroom recording my 4-year-old son Dillon wanting to preach. He had so much passion & was very serious. I sent the video to all my siblings. Sheila texted me back saying "He was going to be a 3rd generational preacher." I had to think for a few minutes. Now wait a minute! If Dillon will be the 3rd & our daddy is the 1st, she was talking about me being the 2nd? I didn't reply back. I just put what she said in the back of my mind. I figured that if she's seeing something about me, she must be speaking 30 or 40 years from now. Boy was I wrong!

The following week, the Black History Month program that I organized was taking place. It was an amazing yet thought provoking program. The message I got from that program was No More Excuses! As I was driving home & reflecting on the message, I began to question "Why black people make excuses? Why black people make excuses?" I kept on saying it so much that I didn't realize that I started saying, "Why I'm making excuses? Why I'm making excuses?" When I realized that I was questioning myself, I knew exactly what that question was about. God caught my attention to ask me, "Why was I running from the assignment He has for me?" My reasonings were because of fear of the opinions of others. He told me, "You can't let other people's disobedience become your disobedience." I told God that I was scared. He reminded me that the best way to prove the devil wrong & get over the fear was to move forward. I said, "YES I WILL! I'M ALL IN!"

The next day, I called Sheila to tell her that I've accepted my calling to preach. She told me, "Oh! I already knew it, Junebug!" It was just a matter of time for you to obey what God wants you to do!" She then reminded me of what she told me the week before. I then told her why I was running from my purpose. She told me that I couldn't worry about what people would say. God doesn't call the qualified, He qualifies the called. Remember, God said touch not my anointed, so if they talk about the man of God, God will deal with them. That was all I needed to hear. Thank you, Sheila! I needed that!

CHAPTER 15

THE BIG DAY IS HERE

The day arrives that I deliver my 1st message. Although the church was packed, there was one person who I was looking for... My Sheila. She was rarely on time, but I felt that she would show up. As service was starting, I saw the front doors of the church opening. Before the person could come in, I could feel that it was Sheila. And it was! I was sooo happy to see her.

After the message, I wanted to thank the people who came & give a special acknowledgment to my favorite & only sister Sheila Prater. Although she was sitting in the back, you could hear her mouth all the way in Mississippi. Lol! We went outside in the middle of the street, talking & laughing like we were kids! The message I gave to them, she said she enjoyed it, but the conversation & silliness she was giving to me, I enjoyed it.

The Prater Kids (2005)

CHAPTER 16

SHEILA'S TRUE LOVE

Now everybody who knows Sheila knows that Sheila **LOVES** to eat. I told her that eating was her ministry. But eating was not the bad part, It was her choices of food that she would eat! My goodness! To Sheila, the greasier, THE BETTER! Yuck! She would take pictures of her food & post them on Facebook. That stuff was so greasy, you had to take 2 boxes of anti-acid pills after you looked at it. And don't forget about the jalapeño peppers. That girl would torture herself eating that hot stuff. After she finished eating that stuff, then she'll say, "I DON'T FEEL GOOD!" I would tell her, "I know you don't feel good! That was enough grease to clog up a drain pipe. As much as we were the same in some areas, our choices of foods were like night & day.

I knew that Sheila loved to eat, so I would invite her for lunch or dinner by posting the invitations on her Facebook page. The majority of the time, she would break our dates. I learned to not take it personal. It wasn't because she didn't care about me, she just had a better offer of eating some old greasy food. She knew that I would go to healthier places & she wasn't in any mood for healthy food! She would love to go out to eat, but hated to come home to get on the scale. She would always tell me to help her eat healthier food, but as soon as a commercial came on with her kind of food choices, she'd changed her mind & tell me, "That's ok, Junebug!" I knew that her weakness was that greasy food. In Sheila's world, Grease IS THE WORD!

CHAPTER 17

SHEILA & HER SAVIOR

As much as Sheila loved to entertain people or just be silly, she was very serious about her relationship with God. There was not a shy bone in her body when it came down to talking about God. She always told people what God could do in whatever situation they were facing. Even if you would call her & she missed your call, her voicemail greeting would fire you up & make you forget about what you were dealing with. There were times that I knew that Sheila was unavailable, so I would call her phone anyway just to hear her words of encouragement.

Sheila not only encouraged you with her words, but she encouraged you with her praise. Anyway she could enhance the service, she would do it. One of the gifts that God blessed her to have was, being an anointed tambourine player. That girl could beat that thang like nobody's business. If the drummer was slacking playing the drums, Sheila could make up the difference. She would make that drummer pick up the pace or go home to practice some more. When Sheila arrived at any church, the people would immediately pass the tambourine her way. Sheila had been playing the tambourine since she was about 4 or 5 years old.

Ever since we were kids, we used to get all the phone books, pots, pans & school books together, & have some church. I played the pots & pans while Sheila played the school books. She played them like she was playing tambourine in mama's womb. Even as we got older, when we used to baby-sit our little brother Walter, we would **"HIGHLY RECOMMEND"** that while we were playing & singing background, he would sing lead, **IF** he wanted to live. Lol!

Sheila was a big supporter to singers & preachers. If someone was singing or preaching & they were not doing a good job, she would clap with her heavy, country hands and cheer them on anyway. But if they were singing or preaching & she was enjoying them, you'll hear Sheila's loud mouth saying "AMEN!" or "SING THAT SONG!" or a big "YES! YES!"

Some of the best times that Sheila & I had was being at our daddy's church. Sheila would be on the tambourine & I'd be on the drums. We would be playing & I would get lost in the moment thanking God that He brought us from being the small kids beating the pots & pans at our daddy's house to playing real drums & tambourines at our daddy's church. About 3 years ago, I had the opportunity to play tambourine with the amazing Sheila Prater! It was awesome. It had been over 38 years since her & I played the tambourines together. We were able to rekindle that moment with our daddy, in the House of the Lord!

Sheila always knew that her help came from God. The thing that many people (including myself) would look forward to, was to go on her Facebook page on Saturday nights, & read her post saying, "Get ready for church in the morning!" or "Don't forget your tithes & offering!" Even though she was as sweet as pie, she didn't want anybody to come in between her & God. Many people had been led back to Christ or to a church home because of Sheila's influence.

Me, Sheila & Daddy (2018)

CHAPTER 18

JUST BEING BIG KIDS

Even though Sheila & I were well into our adult age, when we were together, we would act like big kids. She could make the most stressful times fun. I always looked forward to Sheila & I getting together. She always made me laugh. We would text, call or inbox each other as much as 3-5 times a day. Even in the middle of the night, if she saw the notification on Facebook showing that I was on, she would be inboxing or calling my phone call. She always wanted to make sure that I was getting enough rest & not letting anything or anybody stress me out!

If there were some news or information that Sheila or myself found out, we would be each other's 1st person to contact. Whenever I would tell her something unbelievable, she would say, "OH MY!" That used to crack me up!

I could never have too much time with Sheila. I would even call her to come over to spend the night. That way, we could stay up all night & just be silly. If Sheila wasn't busy or didn't have any plans that next morning, she would definitely be over. Regardless if she's at my place or I was at hers, sleepovers with Sheila were the best! There was never a dull moment with Sheila Prater!

Not only did we have fun in person, but we would pick on each other on Facebook. We wouldn't go a whole week without posting an embarrassing photo or saying something crazy about each other on one another's page. People would always compliment us on our public affection. We would always say, "That's how we really are about each other. How we are on Facebook is how we are in person.". We never hid the love we had for each other & the way we had each other's back. And we wanted everybody to know that.

I used to call Sheila, Ms. Facebook, because she would post some of the craziest stuff you'll ever see. Whenever I would look at her page & it was something that made me shake my head, I would call her & address her by her first & last name, "Sheila Prater? Gurl? What is your **MAIN** problem? Where in the world did you get that mess from? She would always laugh & say, "I have to entertain my fans!" I would often tell her that she needs to be a comic, a gossip or news reporter. I told her that if she became a reporter I would give her the intro: Regular news will tell you the things you need to know, BUT Sheila Prater will tell you the things you DON'T need to know & some stuff you DON'T wanna know. No matter what, Sheila Prater always knew how to lighten the moment.

My favorite month of the year was our birthday month September (Sheila's September 13 & mine's September 16). I looked forward to having the time to honor my favorite & only sister, Sheila Prater. Each year, I would make sure that plans were set for her & I to be together for a birthday dinner. My idea was, if she wasn't dating someone, then we'll celebrate on her birthday. But if she was dating someone, then, I'll let him take her out on her birthday, then I'll take her on the 14th or 15th. As long as we could celebrate between her & my birthday. That way, we could celebrate being the same age as twins, even if it lasted a few hours. What better way to spend her time than being with her favorite brother, on her favorite month & doing her favorite thing... EATING!

Me & Sheila Birthday (2017)

CHAPTER 19

OUR LAST DANCE

One Saturday afternoon, I was home & the doorbell had rung. I looked & saw that it was Sheila Prater. Seeing Sheila was always like seeing a celebrity & I was her biggest fan. No matter where we were at, we were always going to have a great time. She came in & we talked like we hadn't seen each other in years. She was in rare form. That girl had me laughing like she was performing on stage. After we shared laughs, we talked about relationships. Knowing that she was always protective of me, I told her that I would take my time & get her approval on a potential mate. She made it a point to tell me (& others) that she wanted to protect her brother. I told her that I want to do the same for her. She replied with her usual, **"I KNOOOWW!"**

As Sheila & I sat & talked, my internal being was taking photos of every aspect of her & the moment we were in. I looked at her & she looked different. Now, I've seen her all her life & have seen her in many phases, but this time was different. She was radiant & glowing. I said to myself, "Is that Sheila Prater?" I then told her, "Sheila Prater! You're a nice-looking young lady & I don't want you to settle for less than who God has for you!" She said, "Thank you Junebug! I won't!" We talked about future plans. Sheila shared a desire of hers that she wanted to help women.

After I told her that I had started on a project to help, we came up with a plan to work on it together. We talked some more for what seems like seconds, until she was ready to go. I walked her to her truck & tried to stall her from leaving because I really wanted her to stay. I knew that I wouldn't be able to get her back into the house, so I held her door open to talk with her more. This went on for a few minutes until she told me, "I'm fence to go Junebug. But I'll call you later on!" As much as I didn't want her to leave, I knew that I couldn't make her stay. I closed her door, shared

I love yous & saw her drive off. I stayed in the street until she turned on the next street & got out of my sight.

Sheila kept her word & gave me a call. The phone call was just like the other times, yet different (If that makes sense). There were no distractions that could interrupt us. We had one of those transparent, speak from the heart conversations that seemed so bottled up within her & wanted to release it. It was like a weight that was lifted off of her. I was in the place to give back to the one who had given me so much in my life. She sounded like the old Sheila Prater that was fearless. She thanked me for listening & being there. As we were departing from the phone, I said, "Love you!" She said, "I love you more!"

The Sheila Prater

CHAPTER 20

THE DAY I LOST A PART OF ME!

On Sunday morning, March 3, 2019, I woke up extra early to an uneasy feeling. I felt empty, like I had a bad breakup or a void in my life. I figured that whatever that feeling was, that it would pass. Later that night about 9:20pm, I was ending an episode of my podcast show called Breaking Stronghold in Your Life. As I was praying, I heard God say, "The God of Comfort! I am the God of Comfort!" It was such a soft & soothing voice, that those words were stuck in my ears. I figured that God wanted me to tell the audience that He is the God of Comfort.

After I got off the air, I was so exhausted from the long weekend, that I fell asleep before my head hit my pillow. An hour later, my phone rung & it was my nephew Trey. He said, "UNC! MY MAMA WAS KILLED!!" When he told me, I had to think, "His mama? Who is his mama?" When I realized who I was talking to, my heart dropped!" I had to do what no child wants to do… Tell my mama that her only daughter was killed. After I told her & spent a few minutes with her, I went back into my bedroom. I immediately heard in my spirit say, "Pray & thank God for 45 years with Sheila!" Without questioning, I laid prostrated on the floor to pray. As I was getting up, I heard God say, "Now, worship!" Now to some folks, that may sound crazy because I just found out my close & only sister was killed! Nothing was consuming my mind but my Sheila. But I have always believed that no situation should stop you from praise & worship. So, without even thinking about it, my IMMEDIATE response was to go into worship.

As I was in worship, those words came back to me that was said on the podcast… **THE GOD OF COMFORT! I AM THE GOD OF COMFORT!** Then God said, "Although I told you during the podcast, that message was specifically for you!" I was so honored. It was like God was preparing my heart before I received the news. I knew that death (by the way that Sheila died) was NOT God's will. But hearing that God was a Comforter gave me what I needed at that time.

When I was closing my worship, God came in front of me with a paper or diploma rolled in his hand & said, "If you take this charge, I'll be responsible to heal your heart." I grabbed it & asked God for clarity. He told me that the charge was ministering about domestic violence & toxic relationships.

I begin to make calls to let everybody know what happened. This was so unbelievable. I didn't want to lose focus, but I had to check on my mama, daddy, & other siblings. I called my little brother Walter to tell him the news. As I was talking to him, my daddy called. I knew that this was going to be hard, because Sheila & I were always with daddy. I clicked to my daddy's line. To hear his voice begging me not to retaliate broke me down. I promised him that I would NOT retaliate & I would let the law handle it. When word got out that Sheila was killed, the phone started ringing. As cold as it was that night, people started coming over. It was later reported on the news that this particular night was the coldest night of the year. How ironic that the coldest night of the year happened on the coldest night of my life.

CHAPTER 21

FACING THE WORLD, ALONE!

It seemed like it was the longest night ever! I was just ready for the sun to come up. I didn't know what I wanted to do, but I knew that I needed to do something. I was still in shock & trying to wrap my brain around never being with Sheila again.

Now the sun finally came out, I wanted to get away. I figured I'd go to Walmart. Walking around & getting some fresh air may do me some good. Before I left, I posted on Facebook that Sheila was killed! There were instant comments of disbelief. Sheila connected with so many people. Even those who never met us in person reached out stating that they felt like they had a personal connection with her through social media or how they enjoyed me & Sheila's interactions. They knew how much we meant to each other.

I went to my car, headed to Walmart. As I was driving, tears began to flow from my eyes. As I was driving, all I could think about was Sheila. I made it to Walmart's parking lot. I had to fix my face to "try to" look as normal as I could. I eventually got out of the car. As I was walking from the car, I realized, for the FIRST time since I was 11 months old.... I HAVE TO FACE THIS WORLD ALONE!

That was the most *painful* reality that ever came to me. I was the *loneliest* man in the world! It felt like losing a twin, a wife, & my best friend, all in one! The closer I got to Walmart's door, the more afraid I became. I remember walking through the door & everybody was looking at me. As many times that I shopped at that store, I was lost. I was in a world that was unfamiliar. I didn't know where I was going. I ended up at the pharmacy aisle & saw our classmate Vnetta. She ran to me & gave me a hug that I so needed. I broke down in her arms. All she could say was was "I'm so sorry!" & we cried together. Those heartfelt words from a familiar face really helped me in my most vulnerable moment. Eventually,

I was able to pull myself together & thank her for being there for me. After walking around the store for a few minutes, I decided to leave.

As I was walking to the car, I saw another classmate, Shanetta! She gave me a hug & told me how much Sheila & I were loved. Wow! It was like God sent me up there just to get those much needed words & hugs!

I made it back home & was welcomed by many family & friends. It was mentally tough for me to have family or friends to come & they couldn't look at me because they were used to seeing me & Sheila. As time went on, it became a bitter/sweet moment because I too felt their pain, but I was representing Sheila!

I then decided to jump into the shower. While I was in the shower, I had a heart to heart with God. I told God that Sheila & I always celebrated our birthday together. How in the world was I going to celebrate my birthday now? Sheila ain't here no more! Should I quit celebrating it? Then God said, "NO! Keep on celebrating you all's birthdays because you all are just at 2 different locations. So, celebrate via spiritual satellite connection." That gave me a boost of joy that I desperately needed! Then God said, "Remember, I'm responsible for healing your heart!" Thank you, Lord!

CHAPTER 22

JUST SHUT UP!

Throughout the days, I realized that some folks felt like they have to say something to help when a person is grieving, but some folks were hurting me or ticking me off. There were folks telling me, "Be STRONG Man! Be STRONG!" or "I know how you feel!" I was about to lose it! First of all, BE STRONG? Naw! You all are supposed to be strong for us! And to those ones who were saying, "Man, I know how you feel!" I'm thinking, "FOOL! YOU AIN'T GOT NO SISTER! YOU'RE THE ONLY CHILD!"

There are some folks who are not on speaking terms with their siblings, but they are trying to tell me they know how I feel? You ain't got a clue! Even though they may have lost a sister like me, but the kind of relationship they had with their sister was different than mine. So no, they don't know exactly how I feel. The other 2 statements I heard often were.... "She's at a better place or "Well, it was God's will!" Now, I'm ticked off! I thought that my family was going to have to bail me out of jail, because I was ready to chicken choke these foolish people.

Some of them used no wisdom or common sense on what they're saying. There were even people calling me asking me for details on how Sheila was killed or asking questions that I just didn't want to be bothered with. It's just best for them to just SHUT UP! People should think about what they're going to say & who they're saying it to. Some of the folks who said nothing or gave their time, hugs, or presence meant more to me than some empty words from others. I even had a waitress named Cecily from Cotton Patch to come & sit at my table to offer prayers from her & her church. It's moments like those that make a person effective in helping a hurting person.

CHAPTER 23

THE DAY I SAY GOODBYE

As the hours got closer for Sheila's service, I became a nervous wreck. It seemed like my thought couldn't get right. I left home headed to the church alone. All I could do was pray. I told God that I trusted Him & I remembered His promise to me, BUT I DIDN'T FEEL IT & I REALLY, REALLY NEEDED IT NOW! As I was talking to God, He reminded me of the songs that Sheila & I used to sing together as kids (Make it Last Forever by Keith Sweat).

As I began to sing, for the 1ˢᵗ time in many days, a smile came upon my face. My spirit was uplifted & it gave me the courage to continue the drive to the church.

I arrived at the church & there were a sea of cars everywhere. I rushed to park my car & jumped out. When I made it inside the church, people greeted me, but I was trying to find the entrance of the sanctuary. When I finally found the entrance way, as I opened the door, I felt the strength of God ALL OVER ME! I IMMEDIATELY ran to Sheila's casket & felt peace because we were back together again. All I could do was stare at her framed photo by her casket & smile. I wanted to be there forever. I turned around & saw the packed church. I was so honored because they were honoring *my* Sheila. I walked to the back row & started greeting each person in the church. There were people from our old neighborhood, old classmates, families & hundreds of friends who wanted to honor my sister Sheila.

We had a celebration! The songs, music, atmosphere, etc. was fitting for my Sheila. Right before I had words, my little brother was talking & he said something I never realized. He said, "He lost his big sister!" That rocked me! All my life, I always saw Sheila as my "twin", but never realized who she was to other people! WOW! Then, it came time for me to have words about my Sheila. How in the world could I condense a talk on a 45 years close relationship with someone within a few minutes? I had to tell people how much of a hero she was to me & how I wanted to be like her.

As I was telling some stories, laughter went all across the room. Leave it up to me to share some embarrassing stories but I didn't care. I had to be real & speak from my heart. The service was over & we rode to the gravesite. Many people placed flowers on her casket, but I ran to the car to get the brand-new tambourine I bought specifically for her service. I got the tambourine, wrote a personal note on it, laid it on top of her casket & walked away from my Guardian Angel!

Ronnie, Daddy, Sheila, Me- Our Last Photo Together (2018)

SINCE YOU'VE BEEN GONE

Since you've been gone... I had to adjust to this new norm of the reality of not having you here

Since you've been gone... It has been like cutting off a healthy limb, then trying to learn how to operate without it.

Since you've been gone... I realized that you taught me everything about LOVE. From the heart you gave to me & the TRUST you shared with me.

Since you've been gone... I wake up some mornings realizing, I lost more than a sister, I lost a friend.

Since you've been gone... My plans for a wedding will never be the same. Sure, I'll have my BEST MAN, but I won't have my BEST FRIEND!

Since you've been gone... Me seeing a brother & sister interact makes me sad, because they remind me of us. Knowing that what they have, can't compare to what we had.

Since you've been gone... It made me realize that letting God help me with the pain of not having you, was not a ONE-TIME THING, but a CONTINUOUS ONE for when I need it & when I want it!

So, thank you Sheila for 45 of the **BEST** years of my life

I love you endlessly! I've reflected on every moment I had with you & cherish them deeply in my heart... NOW THAT YOU'RE GONE!

The Prater Family with Trey & Tiara (2019)

National Domestic Violence Hotline
Call (800)799-7233
or text Loveis (866)331-9474
www.thehotline.org

Brother Prater
(214)908-3056
P.O. Box 224122
Dallas, Tx 75222-4122
Brother Prater (Youtube & Facebook)
Brotherprater@gmail.com
www.brotherprater.com

Printed in the United States
By Bookmasters